TERRORIST
DOSSIERS

GLOBAL COUNTERSTRIKE

International COUNTERTERRORISM

Samuel M. KATZ

Lerner Publications Company/Minneapolis

Publishers Note: The information in this book was current at the time of publication. However, the publisher is aware that news involving current events dates quickly. Please refer to the websites on page 69 for places to go to obtain up-to-date information.

Lerner Publications Company
A division of Lerner Publishing Group
241 First Avenue North
Minneapolis, MN 55401 U.S.A.

Website address: www.lernerbooks.com

Library of Congress Cataloging-in-Publication Data

Katz, Samuel M., 1963–
        Global counterstrike: international counterterrorism / By Samuel M. Katz.
            p.   cm. — (Terrorist dossiers)
        Summary: Describes the history and current workings of various contemporary counterterrorist organizations in Europe, the Middle East, Asia, and South America.
        Includes bibliographical references and index.
        ISBN: 0–8225–1566–0 (lib. bdg. : alk. paper)
            1. Terrorism—Prevention. 2. Political violence. 3. Police—Special weapons and tactics units.
        4. International police. [1. Terrorism—Prevention. 2. Political violence. 3. Police—Special weapons and tactics units.] I. Title.
        HV6431.K317 2005
        363.32—dc22   2003015415

Manufactured in the United States of America
1 2 3 4 5 6 – DP – 10 09 08 07 06 05

CONTENTS

A'man: an Israeli military intelligence agency

Hamas: a militant Islamic terrorist group founded by Sheikh Ahmed Yassin in 1987

Islam: a religion founded on the Arabian Peninsula in the seventh century A.D. by the prophet Muhammad. Those who practice Islam are called Muslims. Muslims believe in one god, Allah, and their holy book is called the Quran or Koran.

Islamic fundamentalism: a school of thought within Islam that advocates a return to traditional practices and beliefs. Islamic fundamentalists believe in strict adherence to the Quran and Islamic law.

Israel: a Middle Eastern country formed in 1948 as a Jewish homeland. Citizens of Israel are known as Israelis, and the country's official language is Hebrew. Many Jews and Palestinians believe both groups have historical rights to the region that includes Israel.

jihad: an Arabic word meaning "holy war"—a struggle waged in the name of religion. Some Islamic fundamentalists believe they must fight a violent jihad to protect Islam from non-Islamic influence.

Middle East: a geographic and political term referring to nations in eastern North Africa and southwestern Asia

nationalism: a political ideology that strongly emphasizes a nation's culture and interests as more important than those of other nations

Palestinian: an Arab native to the historically disputed region that includes the modern country of Israel

Palestinian Islamic Jihad (PIJ): a militant Islamic terrorist group founded in about 1980 by Fathi Shaqaqi

Palestinian National Authority (PNA): an independent government set up within Israel to administer parts of the country where a majority of the population is Palestinian

Shin Bet: Israel's domestic intelligence and counterintelligence force

special forces: military units trained for special operations, such as counterterrorism

special operations: activities conducted by special forces for particular military or political purposes. Also called special ops, these activities are often carried out in hostile areas and are often covert, or secret.

INTRODUCTION

Darkness fell quickly upon the villages around Jenin, Israel, the full moon barely visible under the cover of the winter clouds. The special forces operators suiting up at a forward base wanted darkness. With night vision equipment, the operators could use the darkness to their advantage. The terrorist they targeted that night would be asleep when his house was surrounded. Darkness would only add to his confusion and fear during the raid. If all went well, no shots would be fired.

For more than a week, officers from A'man and the Shin Bet had been monitoring the movement of the terrorist chieftain, a commander in the Palestinian Islamic Jihad (PIJ). The terrorist was one of the PIJ's rising stars. He had been involved in at least six suicide bombings that killed nearly 30 Israelis and wounded scores more.

But apprehending a wanted man in one of the villages dotting the hills around Jenin wasn't an easy task. Palestinian National Authority (PNA) security services controlled much of the area by day, and the PIJ and Hamas controlled the streets and roads by night. Getting into the village without sparking a full-scale battle would be hard enough. Getting

Israeli border guards cautiously approach a building.

back out with the targeted terrorist commander in custody would be twice as difficult.

The shock of the September 11, 2001, terrorist attacks against the United States reverberated throughout the world. Islamic fundamentalists hijacking four passenger planes and flying three of them into buildings seemed like an awful wake-up call to the intensity of terrorist violence. But for global counterterrorist forces, the attacks only confirmed the dangers they had been combating for decades. Since the 1960s (and even earlier in some countries), terrorist groups motivated by extreme views of religion, nationalism, or politics have waged campaigns of murder and intimidation against elected officials, business leaders, law enforcement officers, and ordinary citizens. The terrorists seek to undermine governments and destroy communities.

Beginning in the 1970s, governments watched this increase in terrorist activities with alarm. They saw that some terrorist groups were starting to work together, creating networks to gather intelligence, exchange weapons and training, and collect money. A new and long-term plan to fight this brand of ruthless, organized terrorism was needed. Terrorists couldn't continue to operate freely, pursued only after their crimes by police and regular soldiers. Many governments began fielding covert and highly trained police and military special operations units to battle these underground terrorist armies.

By the early 2000s, counterterrorist units had accepted a wide and varied set of tasks. Some operations rely on intelligence gathering and surveillance to preempt hijackings, bombings, and other acts of violence. Other operations rely on the physical strength and tactical training needed to stop a terrorist attack already in progress. Counterterrorist units constantly train for any and all contingencies, and they remain on alert, ready to respond to any incident. From the jungles of South America to the streets of Jerusalem, counterterrorist units have faced an often elusive and ruthless enemy with courage and determination.

Afghanistan: a country in southwestern Asia. It was weakened by decades of war when the Taliban, Muslim fundamentalists, seized power in 1992. The Taliban was accused of harboring the terrorist network responsible for the September 11, 2001, attacks in the United States.

Basques: an ethnic minority in Spain. The Spanish government discriminated against Basques for decades, provoking a violent campaign for Basque independence.

Black September Organization: a Palestinian terrorist group founded in 1971

Bosnia: a country in southeastern Europe, formally called the Republic of Bosnia and Herzegovina. In 1992 a civil war broke out among the country's three major ethnic groups, the Muslims, the Serbs, and the Croats. The war ended in 1995, but ethnic divisions remain.

commando: a soldier specially trained to carry out raids

Communism: a social and political theory based on the idea that property and industry should be owned by the whole community rather than by individuals

Delta Force: the U.S. Army's 1st Special Forces Operational Detachment-Delta. Delta Force is tasked with counterterrorist operations outside the United States.

Euzkadi ta Askatasuna (ETA): a violent nationalist group from the Basque provinces of Spain

explosive ordnance disposal (EOD): investigating, finding, and disarming bombs, mines, and other explosive military weapons

Grenzschutzgruppe 9 (GSG-9): Germany's main counterterrorist unit

Groupe d'Intervention de la Gendarmerie Nationale (GIGN): France's premier counterterrorist and hostage-rescue force

Groupe Islamique Armé (GIA): a terrorist group with the goal of establishing an Islamic government in Algeria

Grupo Especiale para los Operaciones (GEO): the counterterrorist unit of Spain's national police force

Gruppo Intervento Speciale (GIS): the counterterrorist unit of Italy's Carabinieri Reali police force

Israel Defense Forces (IDF): Israel's primary security and military organization

Munich Olympics: the 1972 Summer Olympic Games in West Germany, at which 11 members of the Israeli team were killed by Palestinian terrorists. The failed response to the crisis is considered a turning point in West counterterrorism.

North Atlantic Treaty Organization (NATO): a defensive alliance between the United States and European nations formed after World War II (1939-1945)

Northern Ireland: a nation on the island of Ireland governed by the United Kingdom (UK). It was partitioned (separated) from the Republic of Ireland in 1921.

Nucleo Operativo Centrale di Sicurezza (NOCS): the counterterrorist unit of Italy's state police force

Popular Front for the Liberation of Palestine (PFLP): a Palestinian terrorist group founded in 1967

Provisional Irish Republican Army (PIRA): a violent paramilitary group seeking to end British rule in Northern Ireland. Sometimes called the Provos, the PIRA is a splinter group of the Irish Republican Army.

rappel: a method of descending vertical heights, such as cliffs or high walls, by dropping down a secured rope

Red Army Faction (RAF): a West German terrorist group most active in the late 1960s and 1970s

Red Brigades: a terrorist group most active in Italy in the 1970s and 1980s. It wanted to overthrow Italy's government and replace it with a Communist system.

Special Air Service (SAS): Great Britain's military counterterrorist force

special weapons and tactics (SWAT): a term referring to special police units trained to use military weapons and maneuvers

Western: a term usually referring to the governments, economics, and cultural practices of the United States and Western Europe, often called the West

West Germany: a European democracy established in 1949 after World War II. West Germany was reunited with East Germany, a Communist country, in 1990 to create the democratic Federal Republic of Germany.

EUROPE

To Europe, and indeed much of the world, counterterrorism began in Munich, West Germany, in September 1972. Members of the Black September Organization hijacked the 1972 Summer Olympic Games and the international media in the first large-scale terrorist attack in history. Early in the morning on September 5, the terrorists slipped into the athletes' housing at the Olympic Village and kidnapped 11 members of the Israeli team. To demonstrate their murderous resolve, they killed two Israeli athletes on the spot. A global television audience of 100 million watched the rest of the horror unfold.

West German police drop onto the terraces of the Olympic Village in 1972, above the apartment where terrorists are holding Israeli athletes hostage. The terrorists later forced their way out of the Olympic Village, taking their hostages with them.

The West German police and border guards were responsible for security at the Olympics. But West Germany was anxious, even as late as 1972, to show the world that its Nazi history was in the past, that it had become a peaceful country. A large and heavily armed security force prowling the Olympic crowds wasn't what the government wanted the world to see on TV. As a result, Olympic security forces were ill equipped and unprepared to respond to the Black September attack.

West German police attempted a hostage rescue at an airfield outside Munich, where a plane stood ready for the kidnappers' escape. The police tried to ambush the terrorists on the tarmac, but police snipers were outnumbered and outgunned. Their first strike was weak, and the ambush collapsed into a gunfight. During the battle, one of the terrorists lobbed a grenade into the helicopter holding the hostages. The Huey chopper exploded in a huge fireball. All nine of the remaining hostages, one police officer, and five of the eight terrorists were killed. The Black September massacre opened the eyes of many European countries to the realities of modern terrorism. Whether the terrorist conflicts were ethnic, religious, or political, European countries found themselves faced with civilian kidnappings and deaths, bombings of public buildings, attacks on ships and airplanes, and embassy takeovers. These attacks couldn't be countered by traditional police forces, which in some European cities were not even armed. Special forces, carefully trained and quickly deployed, became a necessity.

FRANCE: THE GIGN

There were only two possible outcomes *for the GIGN operators—complete success or complete disaster. The terrorists wanted to die in the name of their holy war, taking all their hostages with them. They wanted to carry out their deadly plan on Christmas Eve. Symbolism is everything in terrorism. But the GIGN counterterrorists had more than symbols. They were armed with submachine guns, stun grenades, and as much adrenaline as their Kevlar body armor could contain. Bursting from their staging areas, they dashed across a frozen tarmac to the besieged airplane. There was no turning back now.*

How and When the GIGN Was Formed

Exactly one year after the Munich Olympics attack, France faced a hostage crisis closer to home. In September 1973, Palestinian terrorists stormed the Saudi Arabian embassy in Paris, taking thirteen diplomats hostage. The hostages were released unharmed, but the incident served as a wake-up call. France had become a convenient European hub for many radical Middle Eastern groups—from Black September to the Popular Front for the Liberation of Palestine (PFLP). France needed a top-notch counterterrorist and hostage-rescue force to protect its civilians. The Groupe d'Intervention de la Gendarmerie Nationale (GIGN) was created on March 10, 1974.

Part of the gendarmerie, or French national police force, the GIGN was designed as a rapid-response force that could intervene decisively in any large-scale terrorist incident. As a police unit, the GIGN is also used in nonterrorist operations, such as prison riots and high-risk arrests. The GIGN has engaged in hundreds of operations in France, Africa, the Middle East, and the South Pacific.

GIGN divers drop from a helicopter into a lake near Evian in southeastern France.

Organization and Training

As the special operations arm of the gendarmerie, the GIGN is under the umbrella command of the Ministry of Defense. The GIGN is organized into four operational groups of fifteen agents and an officer. Two operational groups are specially trained in waterborne operations. The other two specialize in parachuting operations. Two of these groups maintain a permanent 24-hour alert status. The first advance group can be deployed from its base within 30 minutes of being called to action. The second team can be "eyes-on-target" (in position with the target in view) shortly after a mobilization order from the director general of the national police.

The group also has a command and support squad and a negotiation cell (group). The GIGN maintains its own intelligence unit, too, to study potential situations where intervention may be required.

GIGN operators must train to function in a wide variety of terrain and climates. The group covers the diverse territory of France, which is bordered by mountains on two sides and faces both the rough Atlantic Ocean and the near-tropical Mediterranean Sea. The interior of France consists of large metropolitan areas, small villages, and vast agricultural stretches crossed by several major rivers. In addition, the GIGN has been deployed to the deserts and the tropics of other countries.

All GIGN operators are scuba trained and qualified, taught by France's special warfare instructors and combat swimmers. While the United States and Great Britain have special underwater counterterrorist units to protect ships and harbors, France relies on the GIGN to respond if a boat or ferry is seized or a riverside hotel is taken over by terrorists. GIGN operators also receive extensive mountain warfare instruction. All are trained in tactical skiing and cold-weather operations.

All GIGN operators are qualified parachutists. They are taught at the legendary French Jump School at Pau in southwestern France and proudly wear their parachutist wings on their coveralls. GIGN operators usually make five training jumps a year from French air force and gendarmerie aircraft and helicopters. And at least once a year, operators execute a "wet jump," parachuting into deep water in full scuba gear.

Firearms are an important component in GIGN training. A majority of the operators are qualified sharpshooters. GIGN shooters, however, are trained to neutralize suspects, rather than kill them, whenever possible.

Noteworthy GIGN Operations

The GIGN's first major operation was a rescue in the East African country of Djibouti in February 1976. Somali terrorists took 29 schoolchildren hostage on a bus. The terrorists allowed food to be sent in for the children. But unknown to the terrorists, the GIGN had laced the food with mild tranquilizers. This kept the children calm and out of the way while GIGN snipers shot the terrorists. All the hostages were safely rescued.

In France the GIGN provides tactical support for the Direction de la Surveillance du Territoire (DST). DST is France's internal counterespionage and counterterrorist agency, working against foreign terrorists operating in France or in French colonies. The GIGN also supports the Direction Générale de la Sécurité Extérieure (DGSE), the Ministry of Defense agency responsible for military intelligence, strategic information, electronic intelligence, and counterespionage outside France and its territories. GIGN operators usually provide tactical backup for domestic operations—such as apprehending a known terrorist—and many of their operations are executed in plain clothes, where their covert skills of surveillance and quick strikes are useful.

Because of the GIGN's unique makeup—a military force operating in law enforcement—it functions as both a military special operations unit and as a special weapons and tactics (SWAT) force. The group's experience with small-scale covert operations is extensive. In

July 1983, the GIGN rescued hostages held aboard an Iran Air jet at Orly Airport in Paris. The GIGN intervened at the Marseilles airport in southern France in 1984 when an Algerian hijacker attempted to seize an Air France cargo plane. The force has also ventured to New Caledonia (French islands in the South Pacific Ocean) to rescue

A GIGN operator is shown at the Marseilles airport after the 1994 hijacking of Air France Flight 8689.

hostages from island extremists. They have also arrested Basque terrorists in the Pyrenees Mountains between France and Spain.

The GIGN's most famous operation was the rescue of Air France Flight 8689, hijacked by the Groupe Islamique Armé (GIA) on Christmas Eve 1994. GIA terrorists had seized Flight 8689 in Algeria. After executing some hostages, the terrorists demanded that the pilots fly the plane to Marseilles to be refueled. French authorities suspected that the terrorists were planning to crash the fuel-laden jet into the Eiffel Tower in Paris. While Flight 8689 was still on the ground in

Marseilles, the GIGN sprang into action. Using speed and stealth, and backed up by snipers perched in the airport control tower, GIGN operators stormed the plane and freed the hostages. This raid is considered one of the greatest in the history of counterterrorism.

Along with other French security and law enforcement agencies, the GIGN has been heavily involved in combating a new wave of terrorism directed at France. France has supported the Algerian government in its battles against Islamic rebels, drawing the wrath of Islamic terrorist groups. And as in many other countries, the September 11, 2001, attacks in the United States put French counterterrorists on heightened alert. As terrorist organizations develop new schemes for destruction, groups such as the GIGN must continue to develop ways to combat them.

GERMANY: GSG-9

■ ■

The first light of a winter dawn spread over Germany.
The commander on the scene leaned over his communication console, monitoring three sets of radios and speaking quietly into a cell phone. Daylight was a bad time for a rescue raid, but he didn't know if his team could wait until nightfall.

Heavily armed terrorists were holding 245 hostages in an airplane parked in a remote corner of Düsseldorf's airport. The terrorists were demanding the usual—fuel to escape, millions in cash, the release of imprisoned comrades. If the demands were not met, the plane would be blown up with the hostages on board.

The unit operators stood with their weapons, waiting. Finally, the signal to strike came. The commandos rushed to their staging areas. Some climbed inside trucks. Others boarded two helicopters parked behind the airport control tower. Rooftop snipers set their sights on the plane's cockpit.

The negotiators phoned the terrorist ringleader in the cockpit to inform him that the German government had reluctantly accepted his demands. But before the ringleader could respond, a .308 caliber round pierced the cockpit window. It was a direct hit. The ringleader slumped down, still clutching the phone.

The sniper shot was the go sign. The choppers zipped in, and their

GSG-9 operators prepare to breach an airplane door during an exercise.

teams dropped down onto the airplane's wings. The trucks screeched to a stop on the tarmac, and the ground teams leaped out. The rescue force breached the fuselage doors and moved in. The terrorists froze for a moment, wondering if they should detonate their explosives or return fire. They wondered too long. The assault team cut them down with multiple shots. Within three minutes, the passengers were evacuated to safety.

The unit commander was pleased with the practice drill. But as he watched the "dead" terrorists climbing down from the cockpit, he was already making notes for the next training exercise. His unit was on high alert, and what they practiced here could save lives later.

How and When GSG-9 Was Formed

Counterterrorism in Germany rose from the ashes of the 1972 Munich Olympics. After the disastrous attempt to rescue the Israeli athletes, the West German government commissioned Interior Minister Hans-Dietricht Genscher to create a special group to combat terrorism. Grenzschutzgruppe 9 (Border Protection Group 9, or GSG-9) was formed within the Bundesgrenzschutz, the federal border police.

Ulrich Wegener, a counterterrorist expert and 15-year veteran of the Bundesgrenzschutz, is largely credited with GSG-9's organization. Wegener had close links to Israel's commando units and security service. Using an elite unit of the Israel Defense Forces (IDF) as his working model, Wegener was able to make GSG-9 operational in less than one year.

Wegener envisioned GSG-9 as a unit able to respond to any crisis inside Germany and even beyond the national borders if German citizens were involved. According to West Germany's postwar constitution, the regular army was prohibited from operating outside the country. So it became the Bundesgrenschutz's mission to rescue German hostages and diplomats from international hotspots.

For the even more specialized GSG-9, there was to be no challenge that couldn't be overcome—from rescuing hostages on a hijacked airplane to assaulting a Rhine River barge commandeered by terrorists. GSG-9 operators have national authority and powers of arrest. Part of their mission is to infiltrate terrorist groups and learn their plans, so that terrorist attacks can be prevented.

ORGANIZATION AND TRAINING

Wegener divided GSG-9 into three operational sections or combat units. Each unit is further divided into five-person special combat teams (Sonder-Einsatztrupp or SETs). Combat Unit 1 is a conventional counterterrorist hostage-rescue assault unit. Combat Unit 2 is trained in naval special warfare and maritime counterterrorism. Combat Unit 3 is specially trained in parachuting. Nonassault units are made up of technicians, communications specialists, arms experts, trainers, and recruiters.

Also supporting GSG-9 combat units are the pilots and helicopters of the Grenzschutz-Fliegergruppe, Bundesgrenzschutz's flight group. Grenzschutz-Fliegergruppe pilots are considered among Germany's best, trained to land on a dime and fly through the most harrowing of urban and rural obstacles.

■ ■

The operators dangled precariously from the Grenzschutz-Fliegergruppe Bell-212s, low-flying helicopters. Trying to set down on a target that is moving at 100 miles per hour, the operators had to watch for power lines, upcoming tunnels, and other obstacles that could spell certain death. After the team leader lowered himself to the target, he pulled his Glock semiautomatic pistol from his holster and took aim at the entry point. The remaining operators gained their footholds behind him. The attack was under way.

Although it looked like a Hollywood action film, nothing was make-

GSG-9 operators drop from a helicopter during an exercise with the Grentzschutz-Fliegergruppe.

believe about this hostage-rescue exercise. In this scenario, terrorists have seized a high-speed intercity train, taking everyone on board hostage. Unless a ransom is paid and political prisoners released, the terrorists will blow up the train before it reaches the next station.

The GSG-9 operators have no choice but to assault the train as it speeds across the German countryside. Absolute concentration and full peripheral vision are necessary. One lapse and the pilot slams into a bridge or an electricity line. One lapse and the operator loses footing and falls to the tracks. But GSG-9 pilots and operators are trained to hit the target no matter what the distraction or difficulty. In less than 60 seconds, the Bell-212s have maneuvered over the rail cars and unloaded the assault teams.

■ ■

GSG-9 operatives are all volunteers with at least two years' experience as Bundesgrenzschutz officers. Applicants must pass a series of tests for endurance, marksmanship, intelligence, psychological fitness, and physical health. Accepted applicants are sent on 22-week training courses. The training program concentrates on the latest tactics and weapons of both terrorists and counterterrorists. Operators are also trained in such specifics as providing security for high-profile political figures, parachuting, aircraft and train operations, skiing, and first aid.

MAJOR GSG-9 OPERATIONS

GSG-9's first operation was providing security at the 1974 World Cup Games in West Germany. West German intelligence had received reports that the Red Army Faction (RAF) was planning a terrorist attack. German authorities believed the RAF called off the attack because of GSG-9's presence. After this success, GSG-9 was sent to assist security operations at the 1976 Winter Olympics in Innsbruck, Austria, and the 1976 Summer Olympics in Montreal, Canada.

Over the next few years, GSG-9 continued covert counterterrorist operations at home against the RAF. Middle Eastern operatives had also set up shop in West Germany. In 1977 a combined team of RAF and Palestinian terrorists put all GSG-9's training and tactics to the test.

On September 6, 1977, the RAF kidnapped Hanns-Martin Schleyer, a West German business executive. Hostage negotiations faltered, and by mid-October, the RAF was desperate for more bargaining power with the West German government. The RAF made plans for a hijacking operation with the aid of Palestinian terrorists. On October 13, 1977, a Lufthansa airplane filled with West German tourists was seized shortly after takeoff from a Spanish resort area. After days of bouncing

GSG-9 trains for dangerous missions against homegrown terrorists. For years West German political radicals carried out kidnappings and bombings on a regular basis.

INCIDENT AT BAD KLEINEN

GSG-9 was untouched by criticism until one dark summer night in the rural West German town of Bad Kleinen. On June 27, 1994, about 30 GSG-9 operators were on a stakeout with the Bundeskriminalamt (BKA), Germany's federal investigative bureau. They were waiting to arrest two RAF leaders, Birgit Hogefeld, 37, and Wolfgang Grams, 40.

Such police operations were always tied up in German bureaucracy, so several federal, state, and local agencies had to be involved. BKA and GSG-9 agents felt the different officers, tactics, and communications were a bad mix. They were right. During the arrest of Hogefeld and Grams, Grams killed one GSG-9 operator and wounded another before he was shot.

The incident might have ended there if not for the German tabloid press. Eager for a scandal, tabloids reported that a GSG-9 officer had shot Grams in cold blood. GSG-9 operators were cast in the newspapers as trigger-happy Rambos.

Wolfgang Grams was one of the most wanted members of the RAF.

As the scandal grew, some politicians even called for the disbanding of GSG-9. But German chancellor (chief government minister) Helmut Kohl expressed outrage that an RAF terrorist was being portrayed as a martyr.

A month after Bad Kleinen, GSG-9 was deployed to a hijacking situation. A lone Egyptian terrorist had taken over a flight from North Africa to the Netherlands. GSG-9 operators subdued the hijacker and secured the hostages' release without firing a single shot. The unit's ability to handle this situation restored much of GSG-9's reputation. ∎

the plane around the Mediterranean Sea and the Middle East, the hijackers demanded to be taken to Mogadishu, Somalia.

GSG-9 was operational and ready to deploy within hours of the hijacking. Colonel Wegener's operators packed their gear and equipment on a modified Lufthansa Boeing 737 and followed the progression of the hijacked flight until it landed in Somalia. While the West German government secured the support of the Somali government, the GSG-9 task force took off for the rescue assault.

On the night of October 17, 1977, the GSG-9 unit secretly landed at Mogadishu airport, where the hijacked plane sat. The GSG-9 operators knew the element of surprise was crucial when storming the hijacked aircraft. They needed to get all the way to the plane's doors without being spotted. Somali soldiers working with GSG-9 provided a diversion. At 2:05 A.M., only 40 minutes before the terrorists' deadline, Somali troops lit a huge bonfire in front of the aircraft. As the terrorists moved to the front of the plane to see what was happening, GSG-9 operators rushed in, blowing off the fuselage doors and tossing in stun grenades. Five minutes later, all the terrorists were either dead or wounded. The 86 hostages were freed unharmed.

GSG-9 operators became national heroes. The Somali rescue operation seemed to cement GSG-9's reputation and prove the value of maintaining a highly trained and specialized force. GSG-9 remains Germany's domestic counterterrorist and hostage-rescue force, prepared to respond to a variety of crises. Because of its reputation, GSG-9 maintains strong ties to the best of the global counterterrorist community.

GREAT BRITAIN: THE SAS

■ ■

The operators moved slowly but surely through the bogs of *Armagh, Northern Ireland, comfortable with the darkness. Dressed in improvised military gear, they stepped through the rain-soaked marshes quietly, careful not to slosh through the bog's pools and channels. Ahead of them sat a small farmhouse. They would hit the house just before dawn.*

Inside the house were soldiers in the Provisional Irish Republican Army (PIRA), a splinter group of the terrorist Irish Republican Army. The PIRA had masterminded countless attacks against civilians and the security forces. The operators moving through the bog had no illusions about their mission. Their business was as bloody as terrorism itself.

Not everyone had the skill and endurance to reach a target undetected after a three-hour march. Not everyone had the mental strength to sit in the cold and damp waiting for dawn. Not everyone had the courage to burst into a stronghold of armed terrorists. But such is the world of the Special Air Service (SAS).

■ ■

How and When the SAS Was Formed

Great Britain's 22nd SAS Regiment has earned an exceptional reputation in the international special forces community. But unlike the U.S. Army's Delta Force or Germany's GSG-9, the SAS wasn't created as a national counterterrorist force. It inherited the role after the 1972 Munich Olympics massacre.

The SAS dates back to World War II (1939–1945). British army colonel David Stirling revolutionized warfare by inserting small but highly trained and heavily armed units deep behind enemy lines. These units gathered intelligence, organized sabotage strikes, and even carried out assassinations. The 1st SAS Regiment ran covert operations in virtually every campaign theater—from North Africa to the Aegean Sea to Europe.

After World War II, the SAS disbanded. But during the Malayan Emergency (1948–1960), a Communist insurrection in Malaysia, the SAS officially returned to service. Over the next ten years, the SAS acted as a counterinsurgency force in the South Pacific and the Middle East.

Since the 1970s, the SAS has trained and has been deployed as a special operations force. It focuses on counterterrorism, hostage rescue, surveillance, and assault. With demonstrated abilities in both rapid deployment and long-standing assignment, the SAS is perhaps the best known counterterrorist organization in the world.

The winged dagger with its motto "Who Dares Wins" has been the SAS's insignia since World War II.

Organization and Training

The SAS is divided into Sabre Squadrons. Each squadron is divided into four troops of sixteen soldiers. Each troop is a specialized force trained in one type of military insertion (getting soldiers into a particular area or situation). The Air Troops parachute behind enemy lines. The Boat Troops focus on combat situations requiring diving, swimming, or boats. Mobility Troops master driving and maintaining vehicles, from motorbikes to Land Rovers. Mountain Troops specialize in mountain and arctic warfare.

The Counterrevolutionary Warfare (CRW) section of the SAS rotates all squadrons through counterterrorist training and duty. While in CRW, squadrons are known as Special Projects (SP) teams. Each SP team is broken down into Red and Blue Teams, both with snipers and demolitions experts. These units are capable of reaching any location in the world via the Royal Air Force. A "Special Forces Flight" remains on standby at all times.

The SAS is open to volunteers from all branches of the British Army, the Royal Navy, and the Royal Air Force. An SAS applicant must have at least three years' service in a regular unit. SAS selection courses are held twice a year. Fewer than 10 percent of the soldiers applying make it through the selection process.

The selection process begins with a physical endurance test. Carrying heavy backpacks, soldiers march for miles every day in the mountains of Wales. Applicants remaining after this three-week phase enter the "Jungle." This phase tests mental as well as physical endurance. Soldiers spend weeks camping and training, using navigation skills and survival instincts. Next comes the Long Drag, where soldiers again march in the mountains with backpacks and weapons, covering 45 miles in less than 20 hours. Combat survival-training follows, with escape and evasion

Wales has some of Great Britain's most rugged mountains, such as the Brecon Beacons. Special forces recruits march in the Brecons to build strength and endurance.

tactics and interrogation training by former prisoners of war. In the final Tactical Questioning session, candidates are interrogated as if they'd been captured by the enemy.

For those who complete the selection process and join the SAS, training lasts a full year. It includes advanced weapons and assault training and cross-training in other countries. Arctic warfare training takes place in Norway. The Middle East country of Oman is used for desert warfare training. Jungle warfare training happens in Brunei in Southeast Asia and Belize in Central America. Mountain warfare takes place in Bavaria, Germany. Recruits also take courses in high-speed driving, explosive ordnance disposal (EOD) training, hand-to-hand combat, and parachute training.

THE KILLING HOUSE

As part of their training, SAS operators must learn to quickly and efficiently enter a confined space and rescue a hostage from armed terrorists. To create realistic training situations, the SAS built the "Killing House" in Hereford, England. The house can be configured with different furnishings and wall structures, depending on the training situation. Live ammunition and grenades can be used, as the house has walls and ceilings capable of absorbing bullets and shrapnel. Specially hinged doors can be blown off before each practice assault. Mannequins simulate some hostages while fellow SAS troopers take the parts of moving hostages and "bad guys." SAS teams entering the Killing House must learn to quickly determine who is who. Video cameras and instructors monitor each assault so that it can be studied later. ■

MAJOR SAS OPERATIONS

SAS teams have responded to crises throughout the world. One of their longest deployments has been to the troubled region of Northern Ireland. In the late 1960s and early 1970s, violence increased between Loyalists (who want Northern Ireland to remain part of the United Kingdom) and Republicans (who want Northern Ireland to be part of the Republic of Ireland). The violence created paramilitary organizations such as the PIRA. By the mid-1970s, the PIRA's terrorist campaign to overthrow British rule had brought parts of Northern Ireland to the brink of anarchy.

The PIRA had been most successful in southern Armagh, attacking the Royal Ulster Constabulary (RUC, renamed the Police Service of Northern Ireland in 2001). They had also attacked British Army units. In January 1976, the PIRA killed 21 people and overran several army OPs (observation posts). The British government immediately deployed the SAS to Armagh to help the RUC and the army stem the violence

The deployment of a specialized force was necessary to combat the PIRA's well-organized terrorism. Much of the SAS work in Armagh involved observation and intelligence gathering. But the SAS also joined the RUC and the army in ambushes and raids. This experience in combating the PIRA made the SAS one of the world's most respected counterterrorist forces.

In 1980 the SAS made a stunning appearance on the international stage of hostage rescue operations. On April 30, 1980, six heavily armed terrorists from the Democratic Front for the Liberation of Arabistan (DFLA) took over the Iranian embassy in London. They took 22 people hostage, including a Metropolitan Police constable and a British television reporter. Negotiators from the Metropolitan Police began talks with the terrorists, while the SAS staked out sniper positions in a nearby building.

Negotiators dragged out the talks, hoping to secure the hostages' release before an assault team was sent in. But after four days, the terrorists

UNDERCOVER

On the streets of Armagh City or the rural lanes of Loughall, anyone could be an IRA informant. To be successful—and to stay alive—the SAS has to operate in great secrecy or undercover. Sometimes this involves growing out military haircuts, wearing civilian clothes, and hanging out at the local pub, hoping to overhear information. At other times, operators wear camouflage and blackface and wait for days in "hides"—overgrown bushes, attics, abandoned buildings—for a glimpse of PIRA activity. Whenever SAS soldiers gather solid information, they spring into action. Working with the police and the army, the SAS sets up ambushes to stop PIRA operations before they begin, before more civilian casualties are added to Northern Ireland's troubles. ■

lost patience with the negotiators. On May 5, the terrorists shot Abbas Lavasani, an embassy staff member, and dumped his body outside on the pavement. Hearing that the terrorists had begun killing hostages, British prime minister Margaret Thatcher ordered the SAS to move in.

Operation Nimrod began at 7:23 P.M. on May 5. A crowd of onlookers, including the press, watched from behind police barriers as SAS rappellers dropped down the embassy walls. The rappellers broke through the building's fortified windows and hurled in stun grenades. Room by room, the SAS took back the embassy. By 7:40 P.M., five of the six DFLA terrorists were dead, the hostages were free, and the SAS had slipped back into the shadows.

Operation Nimrod took place in daylight on a London street. Crowds gathered to watch, and television crews broadcast the operation live around the world.

The SAS has also engaged in more traditional military operations. In 1982 the unit saw extensive action in the Falklands War, a conflict between Great Britain and Argentina over control of the Falklands Islands in the South Atlantic Ocean. In 1991, during the first Persian Gulf War, the SAS was sent deep behind enemy lines in Iraq to search for Saddam Hussein's Scud (long-range, surface-to-surface) missiles. Also in the 1990s, the SAS was deployed in the violent ethnic conflict in Bosnia, providing intelligence reports. In October 2001, the SAS was sent to Afghanistan, as U.S. and British forces began an attack on the Taliban and Osama bin Laden, the mastermind of the September 11 attacks on the United States. As part of the counterterrorism coalition, the SAS worked closely with the U.S. Army's Delta Force and the Australian SAS.

ITALY: THE GIS AND THE NOCS | Primary

counterterrorist operations in Italy are handled by the Gruppo
Intervento Speciale (GIS) and the Nucleo Operativo Centrale di
Sicurezza (NOCS). The GIS is a unit of the Carabinieri Reali, which was
created on July 13, 1814, as Italy's police force. The police force's
primary weapon was the carbine rifle, from which its name was derived.
The NOCS is a unit of Italy's Polizia di Stato (State Police). Like the
Carabinieri, the Polizia di Stato ensures public safety and enforces state
law. The GIS and the NOCS are also similar in their counterterrorist
missions. Their major difference is jurisdiction: the NOCS operates only
inside Italy, while the GIS can work internationally.

FORMATION, ORGANIZATION, AND TRAINING OF THE GIS

The GIS was formed in 1978, as criminal violence in Italy increased.
During the 1970s, the Mafia, an Italian organized crime group, stepped
up its narcotics trade. To protect the trade, the Mafia threatened and
killed police officials and judges. At the same time, the Red Brigades, a
radical political terrorist group, began a campaign of assassinations,
kidnappings, and bombings as part of its efforts to overthrow the Italian
government. With national security threatened, the Carabinieri
recognized that it needed a unit trained in counterterrorist operations.

The GIS consists of approximately 150 operators drawn from the
1st Carabinieri Airborne Regiment. The unit is divided into three
operational sections and a sniper/reconnaissance team. Each section is
further divided into detachments of four operators. A GIS section is ready
at all times to deploy from base within 30 minutes.

All GIS operators are volunteers. Soldiers and military police
officers serving in the Carabinieri may be considered for the GIS if they
have an exemplary service record. They must also pass an exhaustive
security check into their backgrounds. And to test their motivation,
candidates must pass tests administered by military psychiatrists,
physicians, and senior GIS officers.

For candidates accepted into the program, GIS training lasts
nearly ten months. It runs the gamut of the special operations and
counterterrorist curricula. GIS trainees learn terrorist ideology and
politics. In the field, they train for combat shooting and marksmanship,
EOD, hand-to-hand combat, rappelling and fast-rope techniques, and

combat medical treatment. They also study advanced intelligence gathering and reconnaissance, advanced communications and radio, and basic hostage negotiations.

GIS trainees also learn evasive driving skills. This includes, it has been reported, a week of instruction at the famed Ferrari auto factory and speedway in Italy. The GIS also trains with the Italian special forces Alpini Brigade, learning advanced mountain and alpine warfare skills. Combat swimming is taught by the Italian navy's special warfare unit, the Incursori.

An armed GIS team jumps from a helicopter during an exercise. The GIS focuses its training on high-risk counterterrorist operations.

Major GIS Operations

Italy and the GIS's most serious threat has been from the Red Brigades. Evolved from the ultraradical wing of the Italian labor movement, the Red Brigades quickly moved beyond workers' rights and labor reform. The group's stated objective was the destruction of the Italian government and business sector. They soon expanded their scope to include attacks on North Atlantic Treaty Organization (NATO) personnel and international corporations based in Italy. The Red Brigades exchanged financial and logistical support with other radical groups, including Palestinian terrorists and West Germany's RAF.

The Red Brigades had a large supply of weapons and ammunition, which they'd stolen from NATO and Italian army bases. They were a clear danger to Italian security, and the GIS worked closely with Italian intelligence and police agencies to preempt their terrorist operations. The GIS began a campaign of lightning raids against Red Brigades safe houses and weapons stores. The GIS would isolate and secure a location, then perform an explosive entry. After securing all Red Brigades operatives inside, the GIS would leave, allowing intelligence and police personnel to conduct interrogations and gather evidence for trial.

Between 1973 and 1983, the Red Brigades mounted a remarkable 9,361 attacks resulting in 116 deaths. Hundreds more were wounded. But the threat from the Red Brigades has diminished considerably. Sporadic attacks occur, but much of the GIS's current counterterrorist work involves foreign groups and the illegal drug trade.

FORMATION, ORGANIZATION, AND TRAINING OF THE NOCS

In 1974 the commanders of Italy's Polizia di Stato realized their law enforcement operations needed a counterterrorist tactical unit. Called the Anti-Commando Unit, this force was trained to combat both Palestinian terrorist groups operating in Italy and a violent Communist underground movement. As well as serving as counterterrorists, these superbly trained police officers could execute high-risk arrests against Italy's most dangerous criminals, including the Mafia. The Polizia di Stato recruited about 35 officers from police ranks, focusing on those with athletic experience, including soccer, running, and the martial arts.

After a year of training, the Anti-Commando Unit arrested some high-profile terrorist leaders. In light of these successes, Italy invested more in its domestic counterterrorist efforts and upgraded the role of both military intelligence and internal security bureaus. In 1978 the Italian government renamed the Anti-Commando Unit the Nucleo Operativo Centrale di Sicurezza (Central Security Operation Unit).

The NOCS consists of nearly 50 police officers divided into four 10-person teams. Three teams focus on counterterrorism, while one team is responsible for protecting foreign and Italian dignitaries. Some NOCS teams are on call 24 hours a day, 7 days a week.

During the NOCS basic training course, operators are cross-trained as assault operators, snipers, scuba divers, and EOD experts. Basic training lasts six months, while additional specialized training continues over the course of another eight months. Specialized training includes working with counterterrorist units in other countries.

Major NOCS Operations

The NOCS has taken part in more than 4,000 operations resulting in about 400 arrests. The NOCS has helped combat hardcore organized crime elements in Italy, has protected visiting dignitaries, and has gathered intelligence on many domestic and international terrorist activities.

The group's most significant operation was the 1982 rescue of U.S. Army brigadier general James Dozier, kidnapped by the Red Brigades. Dozier was serving as a NATO officer when he was taken from his Verona, Italy, apartment on December 17, 1981. The Red Brigades announced their hostage demands ten days later. Fearful that the Red Brigades would simply murder Dozier, Italian police forces organized Operation Winter Harvest. In late January 1982, police zeroed in on the Padua, Italy,

Following his release from kidnappers, James Dozier is escorted to a press briefing. Terrorists held Dozier hostage for weeks until the NOCS and Italian police rescued him.

apartment where Dozier was being held. NOCS commandos stormed the apartment and rescued Dozier just as one of his kidnappers was about to assassinate him.

Spain: The GEO

They moved silently, with motions so practiced as to appear instinctive. A dozen officers in black fatigues rappelled down the façade of a five-story apartment block. Once on the pavement, the officers checked their Heckler and Koch P7 pistols and MP5 submachine guns, then raced down the alley toward the building's *rear entrance. The team took their positions without a word, relying only on hand signals and training. The breacher, the operative tasked with breaking down the door, set a square frame laced with detonation cord against the entrance. The explosion turned the wooden door into a shower of splinters. The rest of the team rushed inside. Moving through the building shouting "Policia," the officers fired on any hostile target that appeared. The entry lasted all of 40 seconds. The building was secure.*

A GEO officer gets in position and waits for his signal during a raid exercise.

The group's commander ordered the officers to start the practice drill again—but to go faster this time. For the officers of the Grupo Especiale para los Operaciones (GEO), Spain's elite counterterrorist team, this is everyday work. Doing it again, and better, is part of the job.

■ ■

HOW AND WHEN THE GEO WAS FORMED

For years, terrorism in Spain was virtually nonexistent. Francisco Franco's dictatorship (1939–1975) eliminated most forms of political opposition, violent or not. But by the 1960s, growing economic prosperity and social reforms had weakened Franco and his government.

As Spanish society and government became more open and fluid, the country also began to suffer from many of the problems plaguing the rest of Western Europe. The most troubling of these problems was international terrorism. Middle Eastern terrorists established safe houses and arms stores in Spanish cities for campaigns against Israeli and Spanish targets.

The most pressing terrorist threat, however, came from within. The Euzkadi ta Askatasuna (Basque Fatherland and Liberty, or ETA) is one of Europe's oldest terrorist factions. Formed in 1959, the group adheres to a Marxist ideology, but its driving force is Basque nationalism.

Basque country comprises several provinces in northern Spain, and Basque people have their own language and customs. Franco outlawed the Basque language and cultural practices. Students dissatisfied with more moderate attempts to fight Franco's repression formed the ETA. Even after the reforms of the 1960s, the ETA waged a terrorist campaign against the Spanish police and army. The Franco government responded with indiscriminate beatings and arrests of suspected Basque nationalists. The vicious cycle of violence only worsened.

Highly sophisticated and compartmentalized like no other terrorist outfit in the world, the ETA has been an effective and lethal foe. As the ETA developed, violent intimidation, kidnapping, and assassinations became their primary methods of terrorism. Their targets for assassination include Spanish government officials, officers in the military and security forces, and moderate Basque politicians. The ETA also uses ransom kidnapping and extortion for raising funds. ETA assault squads are among Europe's most capable bank robbers, and ETA bombers are considered to be the world's most innovative and capable.

To counter this threat, Spain's Ministry of the Interior created a national police counterterrorist team in 1977, the GEO (the Special Operations Group). The GEO is responsible for most major counterterrorist and hostage-rescue operations inside Spain, as well as the rescue of Spanish citizens held abroad.

ORGANIZATION AND TRAINING

The GEO is composed of approximately 100 police and military officers. The Spanish government recruits the officers for the GEO.

At its vast training center near Guadalajara, Spain, northeast of Madrid, the GEO trains for every possible terrorist scenario. Every type of building entry is practiced at the training facility, from using plastic explosives on a front door to fast-roping down a building's exterior.

GEO operators use airports throughout the country to train for hijacking and hostage situations. Operators also train regularly for hijacking and hostage situations on passenger trains, buses, and passenger ferries traveling to and from North Africa.

Virtually all of the GEO's training is carried out with live ammunition. GEO operators experience the danger of live fire and feel its power. When bursting through a door to free a hostage or engage a

A breacher attaches a wooden frame laced with explosives to a door. Breaching an entry is the crucial first step in any raid.

terrorist, a GEO operator should have no doubts about how important it is to succeed.

MAJOR GEO OPERATIONS

The GEO has participated in hundreds of operations against the ETA and many dangerous international groups. It kept a very high profile as Spain prepared for the 1992 Madrid Olympics, to discourage any terrorists from even planning an assault during the games. Other GEO operations have been typical of counterterrorism—organizing assaults on safe houses or providing high-level security for terrorist trials. GEO operators have also rescued kidnapping victims and hostages from besieged banks and government offices.

In the last few years, the GEO has been very active against a determined and bloody ETA bombing campaign. They have also used their counterterrorist abilities on the front lines of a major anticrime campaign.

ATTACKS IN MADRID

On March 11, 2004, at the start of the morning rush hour, 10 bombs exploded on four commuter trains bound for central Madrid. The bombs detonated near stations or at platforms, killing 191 people and injuring more than 2,000.

Spain's government first blamed the ETA. But tracing evidence found at the scene, investigators arrested several men with links to al-Qaeda. A videotape from an alleged al-Qaeda leader also surfaced. It announced that the bombs were punishment for Spain's participation in the war in Iraq.

Spain's president, José María Aznar, strongly supported the war in Iraq. His political opponents accused him of blaming the ETA to shift focus away from his pro-war stance. Aznar had little time to respond. At a regular election just three days after the attacks, his party was voted out of office. The new Socialist Party president vowed to end Spanish military involvement in Iraq, a move some decried as giving in to terrorist demands.

Police continued to arrest suspects in the March 11 bombings. But on April 2, 2004, another railroad bomb was found near Madrid and defused. The following day, counterterrorist police surrounded an apartment building in suburban Madrid where several suspects were holed up. Rather than surrender, the suspects blew themselves up. One counterterrorist officer was also killed. ■

Rescue workers rushed to help victims of Madrid's train bombs.

Abu Nidal Organization (ANO): a terrorist group founded by Sabri al-Banna (Abu Nidal) in the 1980s

Arabs: a people who speak Arabic and share a common history and culture. Most Arabs live in the Middle East, but they have also emigrated worldwide.

Yasser Arafat: a leader of and one of the founders of the Palestinian Liberation Organization

Counter Terrorist Battalion 71 (CTB-71): Jordan's primary counterterrorist unit

Fatah: one of the oldest Palestinian terrorist militias, founded by Yasser Arafat and Khahil Wazir in the 1950s

Force 777: Egypt's counterterrorist force

Gaza Strip: a region in the Middle East bounded by the Mediterranean Sea, Egypt, and Israel. Formerly occupied by Israel, the region has been self-governed since 1994.

Hezbollah: a terrorist group based in Lebanon

K-9: a term referring to dogs trained for military or police work

Mossad: Israel's foreign intelligence unit

Muslim Brotherhood Society: an Islamic fundamentalist group formed in Egypt in 1928. Formed as a political party, it developed terrorist offshoots.

Palestinian Liberation Organization (PLO): a group founded in 1964 to represent Palestinian interests. It is regarded by some as a terrorist organization.

al-Qaeda: an Islamic fundamentalist terrorist group founded in about 1989 and commanded by Osama bin Laden

Anwar al-Sadat: Egypt's president from 1970 until 1981, when he was assassinated by Islamic radicals

Sayeret Mat'kal: an Israeli counterterrorist unit specializing in intelligence gathering

Six-Day War: a 1967 military conflict between Israel and the Arab countries of Egypt, Jordan, and Syria. Israel defeated the Arab forces and took over the West Bank and the Gaza Strip.

United Nations (UN): an alliance of countries founded in 1945, after World War II, to promote peaceful international relations and to provide a forum for settling disputes

West Bank: a territory between Israel and Jordan, once part of Palestine. Israel occupied the West Bank in 1967, but in the 1990s, some control of the West Bank was turned over to the newly formed Palestinian National Authority.

Ya'ma'm: an Israeli counterterrorist unit specializing in hostage rescue

THE MIDDLE EAST

Some of the world's oldest and deadliest terrorist groups operate from the Middle East. Hamas, Hezbollah, al-Qaeda, and other violently radical organizations threaten the stability of entire regions. These terrorist groups also attack Western countries, putting more pressure on Middle Eastern governments to respond. But politics, culture, and religion are highly volatile issues in the Middle East. Governments must walk a thin line between responding effectively to terrorism and aggravating the daily violence of the region.

At the heart of Middle East terrorism is the conflict between Israel and the Arab world. Both Israelis and Palestinians believe they have historic rights to the small land between the Jordan River, the Mediterranean Sea, the Sinai Peninsula, and the Lebanese border. After World War II, the United Nations (UN) voted to set up two independent states for both Israel and Palestine. But the Palestinians, backed by other Arab nations, refused the compromise. They believed Israel had no right to the land. Nevertheless, the State of Israel was established in 1948.

Several Arab-Israeli wars followed, with Israel showing political and military strength. Israel gained more land during these conflicts than originally allotted by the UN. With these territorial gains, more than 700,000 Palestinians suddenly came under Israeli rule. Many chose not to live in Israeli-controlled areas and moved to crowded refugee camps in the West Bank, the Gaza Strip, Lebanon, Syria, and Jordan.

Within these camps, Arab anger and frustration took the form of violent radicalism. As compromises and peace negotiations fall by the wayside, that radicalism only becomes more pronounced. Hostage crises,

Jewish schoolchildren wait to disembark a ship anchored at Haifa, Palestine, in 1945. Thousands of European Jews were displaced by World War II. The United Nations sought a solution in creating the State of Israel.

ambushes, revenge murders, and suicide bombers have become daily events for counterterrorist forces in the Middle East.

| EGYPT: FORCE 777 | Many of Egypt's terrorist problems

can be traced to the presidency of Anwar al-Sadat (1970–1981). At first, Sadat was popular. He loosened many of the country's censorship policies and economic restrictions, created a new constitution, and reaffirmed Egypt's ties to the Arab world. But throughout the 1970s, Sadat also reached out to the West, particularly the United States. And he made a commitment to peace with Israel, a long-standing enemy of the Arab world. This upset many Arab nations and incurred the wrath of radical Muslim groups. The Abu Nidal Organization (ANO) and the PFLP vowed to take violent action against Egypt in retaliation for Sadat's relationships with Israel and the West. In the wake of this threat, the Egyptian army was directed to create a counterterrorist unit.

FORMATION, ORGANIZATION, AND TRAINING

Egypt's special forces counterterrorist entity was formally sanctioned in July 1977. It drew its name from that date—Force 777. At first, the unit consisted of a few officers and 40 operators. The unit began from scratch, relying on advice from private consultants and a few international contacts. But Force 777 didn't wait long for its baptism of fire. Libya, Egypt's neighbor to the west, opposed Sadat's moderate policies toward Israel and the West. Through early 1977, tensions between the two countries escalated. Egypt feared that Libya would launch terrorist strikes against it. Force 777 was dispatched into Libya to gather intelligence and run strikes against terrorist training bases. An intense and destructive war broke out in July 1977 but ended quickly with a cease-fire agreement.

In terms of experience, Force 777 was still in its infancy when the Libyan troubles began. The unit had no firm order of battle, no formal rescue experience, and little organization. Force 777 was untrained and under-equipped. Its inexperience showed in severely bungled operations. But the force significantly improved through cross-training with GSG-9, the GIGN, and the U.S. Army's Delta Force.

About 300 operators make up Force 777. They report to the Army Commando Command in Cairo, Egypt. But for many years, Force 777 has kept a low profile. Few details are known about their current organization or weaponry.

MAJOR FORCE 777 OPERATIONS

On February 18, 1978, following a historic peace visit by Sadat to the Israeli parliament in Jerusalem, PFLP terrorists murdered a prominent Egyptian newspaper editor and confidant of Sadat. The PFLP then hijacked a jet in Cyprus bound for Cairo. The plane took off but returned to Cyprus hours later, landing on a remote stretch of airfield under the watch of Cypriot National Guardsmen. To Sadat, the murder of his friend and the hijacking of Egyptian nationals on board the Cyprus plane demanded immediate attention. Sadat ordered Force 777 commandos to resolve the matter.

Anwar al-Sadat was assassinated in 1981. He was gunned down by radicals within the Egyptian army while reviewing a military parade.

The commandos boarded a transport plane from Cairo to Cyprus. But the flight took only one hour—all the time the commandos had to plan their rescue assault. As soon as the aircraft touched down, the commandos were to jump out and race toward the hijacked aircraft.

The commandos didn't know that the Egyptian Ministry of Defense had failed to inform the Cypriots of an impending military action.

When the Force 777 unit landed and began sprinting down the runway toward the hostage aircraft, Cypriot police and soldiers thought the commandos were terrorists. They opened fire, and the confused commandos fired back. In this tragic misunderstanding, fifteen Egyptians and several Cypriots were killed.

A hijacked Egypt Air jet stands empty at Malta's Luga Airport in the aftermath of a rescue attempt by Force 777 in 1985.

This disaster led to many changes in how Egyptian soldiers and counterterrorists are deployed outside national boundaries. Nevertheless, the next time Force 777 was deployed outside Egypt, the operation again ended disastrously. On November 24, 1985, ANO terrorists hijacked an Egypt Air flight to Malta, a Mediterranean island. The terrorists killed five hostages before demanding the release of jailed comrades.

The Egyptian Ministry of Defense immediately deployed about 80 Force 777 operators to Malta. But poor planning doomed the mission. Beforehand, Egyptian military officials did not use any surveillance equipment to locate the hijackers inside the aircraft. Officials reportedly failed to debrief hostages released by the hijackers, and they failed to consult a blueprint of the aircraft. During the assault, the Force 777 commandos used too powerful an explosive to breach the aircraft. The force of the entry blast killed 20 hostages. It is also believed that Force 777 snipers positioned outside the plane accidentally shot hostages. In the end, the botched operation resulted in the deaths of 57 hostages.

Following the fiasco on Malta, Force 777 retreated into anonymity. Little mention of the unit has been made since, although it is known that Force 777 has been active in Egypt's bloody civil war against the Muslim Brotherhood Society. The war against the Brotherhood is, perhaps, the opposite end of the counterterrorist spectrum. It isn't selective warfare meant to save hostages as much as it is full-scale combat. Hundreds of Egyptian police officers and dozens of Force 777 operators have died in the conflict.

ISRAEL: SAYERET MAT'KAL AND THE YA'MA'M

■ ■

The Israeli operators didn't like boat rides. They were far more comfortable jumping out of airplanes at 10,000 feet or marching endlessly through the desert on top-secret missions. But when a secret approach to a North African beach was required, an Israeli missile boat was the only choice of transportation.

The operation's target was a terrorist leader responsible for scores of deaths and planning more. The mission was the essence of counterterrorism—a policy of preemption, acting first to deter terrorists and their leaders. But the operators didn't care about policy. Their sole focus was the target.

The operators made it to the beach landing zone. They met up with naval commandos who'd come ashore hours ago and with a large team of Mossad agents who'd laid the groundwork for the operation. The operators then drove through the congested streets of Tunis, the capital of Tunisia. The targeted location was an opulent, expensive, and well-guarded villa. But the guards wouldn't be a problem. With their weapons locked and loaded, the operators began the attack. The sentries were the first to be eliminated. The target would follow.

■ ■

No nation has dealt with more day-to-day terrorist bloodshed than Israel. Since its creation in 1948, Israel has been at war with Arab

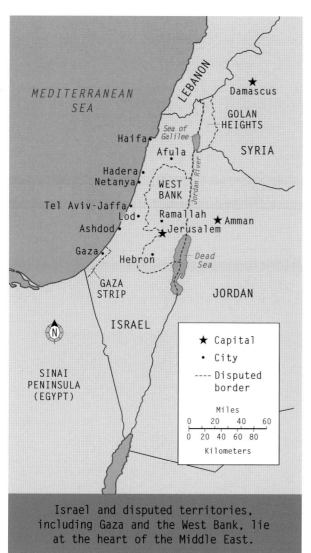

Israel and disputed territories,
including Gaza and the West Bank, lie
at the heart of the Middle East.

governments and terrorist groups opposed to its existence. Israelis face suicide bombings, kidnappings, sniper attacks, and street violence. Outnumbered by its adversaries, the Israeli government has resorted to innovative solutions and sheer determination to counter terrorism.

Israel's counterterrorism philosophy has always revolved around the idea of barriers—intelligence assets and special operations forces trained to stop terrorists at every turn. Israel's intelligence services, including the renowned Mossad and Shin Bet, keep tabs on terrorists outside and inside Israel. Mossad operatives monitor terrorists in their safe havens and bases of operations in the Middle Eastern capitals of Damascus, Syria; Beirut, Lebanon; Baghdad, Iraq; and Tehran, Iran. The Shin Bet has attempted to infiltrate the groups operating inside Israel and in the West Bank and the Gaza Strip. But intelligence operations, no matter how intense and sophisticated, can never completely defeat a terrorist threat. Counterterrorism requires triggers on target and operators trained to fight the most violent opponents.

HOW AND WHEN SAYERET MAT'KAL WAS FORMED

For years, Israel's premier counterterrorist unit has been the ultrasecretive Sayeret Mat'kal, the elite General Staff Reconnaissance Unit of the IDF. Sayeret Mat'kal was created in 1957 to conduct intelligence-gathering forays deep behind enemy lines throughout the entire Middle East.

To carry out these secretive and dangerous missions, the unit's

Israeli police stop a man at a border checkpoint. Checkpoints, vehicle searches, armed guards, and K-9 units are a few of the strategies Israel uses to combat terrorism.

founder, Major Avraham Arnan, wanted to assemble a tough and well-trained force. Sayeret Mat'kal agents had to function undercover in a hostile Arab world. Arnan recruited soldiers who came from poor homes, often the children of Arab immigrants and native Arabic speakers. He sent European Jewish recruits to the desert for instruction by Bedouins (nomadic Arabs) in how to act, speak, and even think like Arabs.

As a rogue force, Sayeret Mat'kal was separate from the regular IDF. Those serving in the unit were released from regular active service in other areas. Sayeret Mat'kal is the best of the best, and it earned that reputation behind enemy lines.

ORGANIZATION AND TRAINING

Sayeret Mat'kal operates in small *tzvatim* (teams). The teams are trained in every aspect of ground combat, and operators are experts with every weapon used in the Middle East. Operators are capable of acting independently of the larger formation, if necessary. Each soldier knows his or her task as well as those of the others on the mission. All of Sayeret Mat'kal's intelligence-gathering operations remain state secrets of the highest order.

Military service in Israel is required, and most Israelis are drafted at age eighteen. Men serve for three years, while unmarried women serve for two years. When an Israeli turns seventeen, he or she is sent to a military center for a series of physical, psychological, and technical examinations. The exams are used to determine if the teenager, once in the military, will be allowed to volunteer for a pilot's course or an elite reconnaissance unit. Many with special talents or qualities volunteer for Sayeret Mat'kal.

All Sayeret Mat'kal volunteers first participate in a *gibush*, or test period. For one week, volunteers face severe challenges. Those who show leadership potential, determination, and strength are accepted into the Sayeret Mat'kal training program. But more than 90 percent of the volunteers drop out during the long and difficult training.

The program begins with basic paratrooper training and jump school. Details of the next phase are classified. But reports suggest that this phase includes highly specialized instruction in all aspects of weaponry, reconnaissance, communications, surveillance, and other "black" (deeply undercover) aspects of special warfare. In all, it takes 20 months of training before recruits qualify as Sayeret Mat'kal commandos.

Sayeret Mat'kal operators are expected to be able to march for hundreds of kilometers, to know how to operate a wide variety of weapons, and to be expert killers. As a result of Sayeret Mat'kal's image of physical prowess, many hopefuls begin bodybuilding when they are fifteen and sixteen. But bodybuilding means little to Sayeret Mat'kal recruiters. One former Sayeret Mat'kal officer explained that the unit is looking for mental strength, not bulging muscles.

MAJOR SAYERET MAT'KAL OPERATIONS

In the 1960s, Sayeret Mat'kal dedicated much of its resources to monitoring Palestinian terrorists outside of Israel. But on May 8, 1972, the terrorists brought their war to Mat'kal's doorstep when Black September terrorists hijacked a Belgian Sabena airliner to Lod Airport in Israel. Holding the passengers hostage, the Black September terrorists demanded the release of 300 prisoners from Israeli jails. Israel refused to negotiate with terrorists, so Mat'kal commandos, masquerading as airport mechanics, stormed the aircraft to rescue the hostages.

Four years later, Sayeret Mat'kal spearheaded an operation that

Rescued hostages are led to safety after the 1972 hijacking of a Sabena airliner. Some of the Sayeret Mat'kal commandos are still wearing the white mechanics' coveralls they donned as disguises to approach the terrorist-held plane.

remains the most spectacular hostage rescue in history: the raid on Entebbe, Uganda. On June 27, 1976, an Air France flight from Tel Aviv, Israel, to Paris, France, was taken over by four armed hijackers—a German man and woman with connections to the RAF, and two PFLP men. The hijackers demanded that the flight be flown to Africa. After refueling in Libya, the plane went on to Uganda, where the four hijackers were joined by more PFLP terrorists. The terrorist group had the full cooperation of Ugandan president Idi Amin and his military.

At the airport in Entebbe, then Uganda's capital, the terrorists separated the Jewish hostages from the others. The Israeli government feared that the Jews would be murdered. The government turned to Mat'kal and the IDF, and Operation Thunderball was put in motion. On July 3, 1976, Mat'kal commandos and several IDF reconnaissance units were dispatched to Uganda aboard C-130 Hercules transports. The Israeli assault force managed to land unnoticed at Entebbe. The commandos stormed the airport terminal building where the hostages were being held and killed the terrorists and their Ugandan accomplices.

Before and after Entebbe, Sayeret Mat'kal ventured on dangerous counterterrorist missions. Sayeret Mat'kal commandos have assassinated top Palestinian terrorist commanders in Beirut and Tunis. They have also been operational against Hezbollah in Lebanon and against Palestinian terrorist groups inside the Gaza Strip and the West Bank.

How and When the Ya'ma'm Was Formed

Israel's national hostage rescue and counterterrorist unit is the Ya'ma'm— the Hebrew acronym for the Yechida Mishtarteet Meyuchedet (Special Police Unit). In 1972 Israeli security officials noticed an alarming trend in terrorist attacks. They were growing bolder and larger in scale, and they almost always involved hostages. In early 1973, the Mishmar Ha'Gvul (National Police Border Guards) ordered the creation of the Ya'ma'm.

The Ya'ma'm's importance to Israel's counterterrorist battle greatly increased in 1974, following a disastrous hostage rescue at Ma'alot High School in northern Israel. On May 15, 1974, Palestinian terrorists took more than 100 students and teachers hostage inside the school. Sayeret Mat'kal was called in to end the crisis, but their rescue plan quickly went awry. A gun battle ensued. All the terrorists were killed, but so were 21 students and four adult civilians. Following the

A Sayeret Mat'kal commando rescues a teenage hostage during the massacre at Ma'alot High School in 1974.

Ma'alot disaster, Israeli prime minister Golda Meir authorized the formation of a governmental commission to define the areas of responsibility between the police and the IDF in handling terrorist attacks. The government authorized the Israeli National Police to assume responsibility for all internal security and terrorist matters. The Ya'ma'm was named the national counterterrorist and hostage rescue force.

ORGANIZATION AND TRAINING

The Ya'ma'm is believed to consist of approximately 200 operators. Like Sayeret Mat'kal, the Ya'ma'm is built around tzvatim. Each team is divided into specific sections, including an entry team, rappellers and climbers, snipers, a K-9 team, and an EOD team. The unit also fields a separate intelligence element.

To be eligible to volunteer for the Ya'ma'm, a candidate must be between the ages of 21 and 28 and must have successfully completed service in the IDF. The Ya'ma'm prefers those who have served in combat and elite special operations units and those who have completed command courses, such as sergeants and officers. To begin training with the Ya'ma'm, candidates must pass grueling physical and psychological testing.

Ya'ma'm commandos practice a raid on a building.

Ya'ma'm training lasts a little over one year. The first eight months are basic counterterrorist training completed by all new members to the unit. The rest of the training focuses on specialty instruction, such as explosives, dog handling, and sniping.

MAJOR YA'MA'M OPERATIONS

The Ya'ma'm's first real counterterrorist operation came on March 11, 1978. Terrorists from Force 17, an elite group within Yasser Arafat's Fatah faction, landed on Israel's Mediterranean coast and commandeered a bus full of passengers headed to Tel Aviv. At the Country Club Junction, just north of the city along the bustling coastal highway, Israeli police and military units, including the Ya'ma'm, set up a roadblock. As the Ya'ma'm readied itself for a rescue assault, one of the hostages attempted to overpower a terrorist. Shots rang out, and a grenade detonated prematurely. Fearing that the terrorists would execute the hostages, the Ya'ma'm made its move. Thirty-seven hostages were killed in the melee and nearly 70 wounded. All the terrorists were either killed or captured.

The Country Club Junction Massacre, as the incident was called, was a tragic beginning for the Ya'ma'm. But by the early 1980s, the unit developed into a top-notch fighting force. During Israel's 1982 invasion of Lebanon to destroy terrorist bases there, the Ya'ma'm was regarded as Israel's premier counterterrorist force. The unit operated in Lebanon as the Shin Bet's tactical arm, executing high-risk raids against terrorist fugitives hiding in caves and refugee camps. The Ya'ma'm was behind the seizure of many of the most wanted and notorious Palestinian terrorists, including Azmi Zerayer, who was considered the most brutal of Arafat's Palestinian Liberation Organization (PLO) chieftains in Lebanon.

In March 1988, the Ya'ma'm once again faced a bus hijacking. Early in the morning on March 7, 1988, three heavily armed members of Force 17 crossed the Egyptian-Israeli border and made their way into the Negev Desert. There they seized a bus carrying workers, mostly middle-aged women, to their jobs at a nuclear reactor in southern Israel. The hijackers drove the bus to a secluded stretch of desert highway. The Israeli government opened negotiations, but talks failed, and the terrorists began executing hostages. The Israeli government brought in the Ya'ma'm. Ya'ma'm snipers killed the terrorists and rescued the remaining hostages.

The "Bus of Mothers" incident made the Ya'ma'm famous, but its

A Ya'ma'm team breaks into a house in the West Bank held by Israeli right-wing settlers. The far right believes Jewish religious law should govern Israel. Like Arab extremists, they are a threat to Israeli security.

reputation as a world-class counterterrorist force was earned over the long haul. The unit fought ceaselessly against Hamas and the PIJ from 1992 to 1997. During the al-Aqsa Intifadah, a violent Palestinian uprising in the West Bank in 2000, the Ya'ma'm again operated nearly 365 days a year against the most fanatical terrorists Israel had ever faced.

■ ■

Marwan Za'iya was known as the worst of the worst—
a terrorist even the Palestinians feared for his cruelty. This Hamas
commander was personally responsible for the murder of 24 Israelis
and Palestinians. The Israelis decided his bloody career in Gaza had
to be stopped. The task was given to the Ya'ma'm.

It wouldn't be easy. Za'iya's home sat in the center of an
overcrowded complex of connecting apartments. During the day, the
complex's common areas were filled with women and children. Any
tactical deployment amid a civilian population is dangerous. But
when the civilians are hostile to police and are on their home turf, a
deployment could easily turn deadly for many innocents.

The Ya'ma'm task force knew what they were facing when they reached Za'iya's building early on the morning of May 21, 1992. Za'iya and other terrorists saw the Ya'ma'm coming and quickly escaped up the building's stairs. One Ya'ma'm team, led by Sergeant Major Eran Sobelman, followed the terrorists. But Sobelman hesitated momentarily when he saw a crowd of old women and small children. During that moment of hesitation, Sobelman was killed by a gunshot to the head from one of the terrorists. The building was quickly surrounded as reinforcements arrived on the scene. The Ya'ma'm killed the terrorists and secured the building, but not before one of the Ya'ma'm had paid the ultimate price.

■ ■

In the fight against Hamas, the PIJ, and other Palestinian terrorist groups, the Ya'ma'm raid safe houses where suicide bombers are prepped for their deadly missions. The unit also intervenes when suicide bombers are tracked down before striking.

On March 3, 2000, the Ya'ma'm was summoned to Taibeh, a city of 35,000 in the West Bank. The night before, the Shin Bet received information from Palestinian collaborators that a group of terrorists in Taibeh were preparing for major attacks in Tel Aviv. At 5:00 A.M., the Ya'ma'm surrounded the house. Since there were no hostages, there was no rush to assault the building. Instead, the Police Negotiation Unit called for the terrorists to surrender. But only one man, having second thoughts about martyring himself, emerged from the house. A few hours into the siege, two more terrorists came out holding a suitcase. They started toward the Ya'ma'm operators, and suddenly one of them drew a handgun. The Ya'ma'm opened fire, killing the two terrorists. The suitcase exploded, injuring an operator.

No discernible movement took place inside the house for several more hours. A Ya'ma'm K-9 dog was sent in to search the building for more explosives. The dog found one charge, which exploded and killed him. Not willing to risk any more dogs, the operators sent in a police EOD robot to test suspicious objects. The robot found nothing more. An armored IDF bulldozer was then brought in to destroy the house. The operation ended when one last terrorist fired at the bulldozer before being killed by a Ya'ma'm sniper.

MISTA'ARVIM

Perhaps the most unique of all Israel's forces, personifying its innovative approach to counterterrorism, are its undercover or "Arabist" units. These units, known as Mista'arvim, are designed to masquerade as Palestinians to gather intelligence or execute small-scale strikes. The first Mista'arvim date back to 1909 and the Shomer, an organization designed to provide security to the first Jewish settlements in Palestine. Shomer guards rode Arabian horses, wore traditional Arab garments, and spoke fluent Arabic. By infiltrating Arabic communities, the Shomer could watch for suspicious behavior and overhear any anti-Jewish plans. Israel continued to develop Arabist units, including Sayeret Rimon in the 1970s, Duvdevan in the 1980s, and the Ya'mas in the 1990s.

The primary objective of these undercover squads was to hunt down wanted terrorists. Training is lengthy and dedicated to intelligence work and the art of undercover operations. The "Arabization" of the operator, from learning traditional customs and culture to intensive language instruction, is extensive. The undercover operators must learn to think in Arabic and function as Arabs. Only once the operator has mastered his new identity can intensive combat instruction begin. ■

JORDAN: CTB-71

*By **midmorning**, temperatures had reached 120°F. But the heat, the scorching desert sun, the heavy fatigues and body armor—these didn't deter the Jordanian operators. Their job was to assault an isolated two-story structure where terrorists were hiding. The terrorists were probably asleep—desert dwellers usually rest when the sun is strongest—and their guard was down. The first operator was wrapped in Kevlar and a bomb disposal suit. As the breacher, the first through the door, it was his job to absorb enemy gunfire and get the rest of the team in.*

The commander watching the exercise unfold wasn't concerned by the climate or by the operator's comfort. There was a job to do, and his unit was in the business of results. Counterterrorism was what he demanded of his men, and it was what his king demanded of him.

The Kingdom of Jordan lies in the middle of the Middle East. As with many of its neighbors, Jordan's population is largely Arab and Muslim. But Jordan's interests have not always coincided with its neighbors' policies. For decades, Jordan has been considered a moderate Arab country with important ties to the West. This has often made its position in the Middle East a challenge.

Jordan's history with its only non-Arab neighbor, Israel, has been marked by wars and frequent border skirmishes. Yet other Middle Eastern countries have accused Jordan of being too tolerant of Israel. Jordan belongs to the Arab League, an organization formed to strengthen ties among Arab countries. Yet other Arab League members Syria, Iraq, and

A burned-out jet sits on an airfield in Jordan, the result of a terrorist bombing. Jordan struggles with its position as a moderate Arab country in the center of Middle East violence.

Saudi Arabia have had ongoing hostilities with Jordan. Internally, Jordan's stability is threatened by Palestinian guerillas and terrorist organizations, even though Jordan is the only Middle Eastern country to grant citizenship to Palestinian refugees from the West Bank. Given these external and internal threats, Jordan's military has focused on defensive strategies.

HOW AND WHEN CTB-71 WAS FORMED

Jordan's primary counterterrorist unit is the Royal Jordanian Special Operations Command's Counter Terrorist Battalion 71, or CTB-71. The unit traces its origins to the outcome of the 1967 Six-Day War. Israel dealt Arab foes a serious defeat, driving some Palestinian groups in Jordan to more radical and violent tactics. More than half of Jordan's population was Palestinian, and the PLO and other guerrilla groups took control of large parts of the country. Jordan's King Hussein began to fear that the guerrillas planned to topple his government. By late summer 1970, what amounted to a civil war had broken out in Jordan.

Fighting continued into what became known as Black September. The Jordanian army destroyed many guerrilla bases and drove many terrorists out of the country. But the terrorists regrouped in Lebanon. There, a radical Palestinian group adopted the name Black September. In November 1971, the group assassinated Hussein's prime minister, Wasfi Tal, at a Cairo, Egypt, hotel. CTB-71 was formed in response. In September 1972, Black September perpetrated the Munich Olympics Massacre. Jordan, like many other countries, recognized the urgency in preparing its counterterrorist forces.

ORGANIZATION AND TRAINING

CTB-71 is a small and cohesive force of operators. They are the best fighters in Jordan's special forces—the smartest and toughest soldiers, with the strongest leadership qualities and natural skills in innovation and improvisation.

CTB-71 is believed to consist of about 100 operators. It is made up solely of volunteers from local ethnic groups—mainly Bedouins and Circassians. In the early 1990s, the counterterrorist team was upgraded to a national force, under the command and control of the Ministry of Defense and General Staff.

Getting into CTB-71 is not easy. Next to becoming a combat pilot, it is one of the most difficult and coveted duties in the Jordanian military. The sole path to CTB-71 is a long one, running through conventional special forces. Only the very best of the special forces are allowed to apply to "71."

Applicants must pass a grueling series of physical and psychological examinations. Subsequent training includes basic military drill, physical training, and forced marches. In the field and in the classroom, trainees learn navigation, topography, map reading, basic signals and communications, and emergency medical care. They then train in many specialized areas, including advanced weapons, antitank operations, mountain warfare, amphibious operations, martial arts, hand-to-hand combat, and riot control.

After graduating from the Special Forces School, the commando enters another phase of instruction where newly mastered skills are put to use in squad, platoon, and company exercises. Working with different units and support services, commandos practice tactical parachuting, urban warfare, and airborne operations.

Graduates of the basic commando course become full-fledged members of the airborne battalion. Following several years of service with an

A Jordanian commando wears a ghillie suit in the field. Ghillie camouflage mimics leaves and foliage.

exemplary record, the best soldiers from the battalion are allowed to volunteer into the Special Forces Battalion, which includes CTB-71.

MAJOR CTB-71 OPERATIONS

Virtually all the unit's operations are classified. But often the unit is involved in operations to prevent armed terrorists from setting up shop in Jordan or using the country to stage attacks against Israel. CTB-71 is tasked with being able to respond to any—and every—terrorist and hostage-taking incident inside Jordan and even to incidents beyond the national frontiers. These scenarios include assaults on hotels, government offices, embassies, and other sensitive targets seized by terrorists.

CTB-71 analysts and computer specialists investigate almost every target of note inside the country. They produce computerized images and graphics, including blueprints. They can even determine the thickness of walls and windows in terrorist hideouts.

CTB-71 operators are also well versed in the tubular assault, the hostage-rescue technique used on buses, airplanes, or other "tube"-shaped vehicles. Aircraft hijackings particularly concern CTB-71, since Black September and Hezbollah have both targeted Royal Jordanian Airlines. CTB-71 routinely takes over a corner of Queen Alia International Airport to hone its skill in aircraft takedowns. The unit trains extensively in different kinds of cabin assaults.

Despite the image of the Royal Jordanian Special Forces operator as an elite expert in desert operations, CTB-71 also combats maritime terrorism. All CTB-71 operators are qualified in scuba diving, as Aqaba, Jordan's only seaport, is a coveted strategic target for terrorists.

A CTB-71 team practices surrounding and securing a passenger bus. Jordanian security forces specialize in tubular assault rescues.

When he was head of the Royal Jordanian Special Operations Command, then Prince (later king) Abdullah internationalized CTB-71 in terms of its contacts and equipment. He contacted some of the best units around the world—U.S. Delta Force, the SAS, GSG-9, and the GIGN. CTB-71 also reached out to some of the newer units in the field that required Jordanian expertise and assistance.

OTHER INTERNATIONAL FORCES

Virtually every nation—from small, economically underdeveloped countries to the industrial giants of Europe—fields units capable of combating terrorist threats. Some of the most prominent are included here.

AUSTRALIA: THE SAS

The Australian Special Air Service dates back to World War II, when the Australian Army organized and deployed commando units to work behind Japanese lines. Modeled after its British counterpart, the Australian SAS uses the same regimental badge (a winged dagger) and motto ("Who Dares Wins").

In recent years, the SAS has been deployed to East Timor, an island north of Australia. In 1975 Indonesia invaded East Timor, brutally repressing

Australian SAS commandos assault a building during exercises at a defense facility near Sydney, Australia, in May 2003.

any East Timorese independence movements. In the late 1990s, Australia sent in both peacekeeping troops and special forces to gather intelligence on Indonesian military plans.

Australia was also one of the first nations to join the U.S.-led war against terrorism after September 11, 2001. Both the SAS and regular troops were deployed to Afghanistan. In October 2002, al-Qaeda retaliated against Australia by bombing a nightclub on Bali, an island in Indonesia popular with tourists. Eighty-eight Australians were killed. In the aftermath of the Bali bombing, Australian prime minister John Howard announced that the country's special forces would add soldiers and expand its mission.

The Australian SAS joined the U.S.-led coalition in Iraq in 2003. SAS units captured Iraqi military bases and weapons, engaged Iraqi forces loyal to Saddam Hussein, and patrolled and secured Iraqi towns.

CANADA: JTF-2

The Canadian government doesn't officially admit having an elite counterterrorist force, but information about it has appeared in the media. In 1993 the Department of Defense took over the Royal Canadian Mounted Police's special response team and formed Joint Task Force 2 (JTF-2). JFT-2 is responsible for all federal-level counterterrorist and hostage rescue operations. It is also assigned to missions anywhere in the world if Canadian national security is threatened. Although the unit's size remains classified, it is known that JTF-2 contributed 40 operators to the war against al-Qaeda in Afghanistan. As part of Task Force K-Bar in Afghanistan, JTF-2 operators participated in many mountaintop surveillance missions. They also searched caves being used as terrorist bases.

COLOMBIA: AFEAU

Colombia is known for both its political terrorism and a violent drug trade, and several counterterrorist units operate in the country. The primary hostage rescue and counterterrorist unit is the Agrupacion de Fuerzas Especiales Anti-Terroristas Urbanas (Urban Anti-terrorist Special Forces, or AFEAU). AFEAU was formed in 1985 in response to increased guerrilla attacks in Colombia. The unit is made up of approximately 100 volunteers from all branches of the armed forces and the national police.

India: NSG

The lead counterterrorist unit in India is the National Security Guards (NSG). The NSG is known as the Black Cats because of their black fatigues and masks. The unit was created under the National Security Guard Act of 1985. The Black Cats are responsible for direct-action assaults against terrorist targets inside India. They also specialize in hostage rescue, dignitary protection, and anti-hijacking interventions.

Counterterrorist soldiers guard the Akshardham Temple in Gandhinagar, India, in October 2002. Terrorists attacked the Hindu temple on September 24, 2002, killing 30 people.

The Netherlands: The BBE

Counterterrorism in the Netherlands is the domain of the Bijzondere Bijstands Eenheid (Special Interest Force, or BBE). The BBE is the special operations force of the Royal Netherlands Marine Corps. It was organized after the 1972 Munich Olympics. In addition to counterterrorism, the BBE has handled hostage rescues at prisons, in schools, and aboard trains. The unit is controlled by the Ministry of Justice for operations inside the Netherlands, but it has operated overseas. In Afghanistan the BBE joined forces with U.S. and British units to fight al-Qaeda.

During a training exercise, a BBE unit uses tanks to assault a hijacked passenger train.

PAKISTAN: THE SSG

Responding to serious terrorist strikes in Pakistan is the task of the army's elite Special Services Group (SSG). Trained by the British SAS, SSG commandos handle raids, hijackings, and hostage situations. Since 2001 SSG has been involved in disrupting al-Qaeda operations along Pakistan's border with Afghanistan.

PERU: FOE

Peru's Fuerza de Operaciones Especiales (Special Operations Force, or FOE) is the army's elite hostage rescue force. FOE has waged a relentless campaign against Peru's Communist rebels, including the remarkable rescue of hostages from the Japanese ambassador's residence in Lima in 1997.

Peruvian special forces guard a financial center in Lima, Peru, during the 2001 Iberoamerican Summit. The Peruvian government feared terrorists would attack the annual meeting of North and Latin American leaders.

POLAND: GROM

Poland's national counterterrorist team is the army's Grupa Reagowania Operacyjno Mobilnego (Operational Mobile Response Group, or GROM). The first GROM unit was selected and trained in 1991. GROM trains year-round in settings as realistic as possible. Given Poland's large size and diverse terrain, GROM prepares for all types of terrorist scenarios. It also has foreign experience in the Balkans, Lebanon, Haiti, and Afghanistan. In 2003 GROM joined coalition forces in Iraq.

RUSSIA: ALPHA GROUP

In 1974, in the aftermath of the Munich Olympics, the Soviet Union authorized the creation of a counterterrorist and hostage rescue unit. The force was initially called Group A but eventually became known as the Alpha Group. Ironically, the Communist and anti-Western Soviet Union had long supported and trained many of the world's terrorist groups. It gave Black September significant logistical support in preparing for and executing the Munich Olympics massacre.

After the collapse of the Soviet Union in 1991, Russia became an independent democratic country. But the breakup of the Soviet Union, with its iron grip on politics and culture, left a void. Many ethnic clashes and territorial disputes arose. In response, Alpha Group has developed into one of the world's busiest counterterrorist units.

Alpha Group has seen extensive action in Chechnya, a republic in southwestern Russia. Chechens, Chechnya's largest ethnic group, are Muslim and have long resisted Russian rule. In 1994 Chechnya declared itself independent, but Russia ignored the declaration. Subsequent fighting between forces has resulted in thousands of deaths. Alpha Group's role in the conflict has been to execute raids against Muslim extremists.

On October 23, 2002, a hostage crisis brought the Alpha Group to prominence in world news. About 40 heavily armed Chechen rebels burst into a theater in Moscow, the Russian capital, during a musical performance. Taking about 700 audience members and performers hostage, they announced that they would blow everyone up if police stormed the theater. The rebels freed children and Muslim audience members, who reported to police that the rebels were demanding an end to Russia's war in Chechnya. Negotiations with the government stalled after three days. Alpha Group was called in to end the crisis.

A gas meant to disorient and incapacitate the terrorists was released into the theater. In the ensuing rescue, all the terrorists were

Russian special forces wait outside a Moscow theater where Chechen rebels hold 700 hostages, in October 2002. The rebels threatened to blow up the theater if authorities attempted a rescue.

killed. But rescuers misjudged the amount of gas released into theater, and many of the hostages were poisoned. More than 100 died. Authorities were criticized for the civilian casualties of the rescue, but many Russian people expressed support for the action.

SOUTH KOREA: 707TH SPECIAL MISSIONS BATTALION

South Korea's elite 707th Special Missions Battalion (707) is part of the South Korean army's Special Forces Unit. Established after the Munich Olympics, 707 responds to any terrorist threat inside South Korea or overseas if South Korean hostages are involved. The 707 has 200 soldiers divided into two companies. Each company is composed of teams of 14 operators and their commanders. Reportedly, the 707 also maintains a group of combat-trained women who infiltrate certain situations, such as posing as nurses or flight attendants during a hijacking.

South Korean special forces stand guard during counterterrorism exercises at a soccer stadium in Seoul, South Korea, in February 2002. South Korea hosted the 2002 World Cup tournaments.

EPILOGUE*

Early in 2004, attacks against civilians rocked Europe. In February a suicide bomber attacked a Moscow, Russia, subway train, killing 39 and wounding 120. Russian president Vladimir Putin blamed Chechen rebels. In March the deadly bombing of several Madrid commuter trains devastated Spain. Spanish authorities blamed North African terrorists, possibly connected to al-Qaeda.

In the Middle East and South America, civilians have long been in the cross fire between terrorists and government forces. But terrorists intentionally attacking public transportation, office buildings, tourist sites, and stores is becoming more common. Counterterrorists see an ominous pattern in this spread of attacks on civilian "soft targets."

Some soft targets have symbolic value for terrorists. Counterterrorists are very concerned, for example, about possible attacks on the September 2004 Olympic Games in Athens, Greece. In February 2004, the Greek government took the unprecedented step of asking NATO troops to help guard the Olympics.

At the Olympics, the police and military can rely on state-of-the-art communications, metal detectors, K-9 units, and patrols. But in more common attacks on soft targets, the challenges are enormous. Soldiers and police cannot guard every city bus or corner grocery store. Instead, counterterrorists increasingly rely on intelligence and monitoring to prevent attacks. In March 2004, European and U.S. counterterrorist officials revealed a dramatic example of intelligence technology. Investigators showed how they had used tiny Swiss cell phone chips to track the conversations and movements of al-Qaeda agents for two years.

The U.S.-led war on terror also continues to rely on the strategy of removing terrorist leadership and sources of revenue. In February 2004, international counterterrorist forces began a new push to find fugitive al-Qaeda leader Osama bin Laden. British SAS, U.S., and Afghan units swept the mountains between Afghanistan and Pakistan. British and U.S. military intelligence believe bin Laden and senior al-Qaeda leaders are hiding in the mountains. On the other side of the border, thousands of Pakistani troops block escape routes. In March this hunt for al-Qaeda leaders resulted in a fierce weeklong gun battle between Pakistani troops and Muslim radicals. Israel also continued to target terrorist leaders. On March 22, 2004, Israeli troops killed Hamas founder Sheikh Ahmed Yassin in an air strike in the Gaza Strip. ■

*Please note that the information in this book was current at the time of publication. To find sources for late-breaking news, please see page 69.

Timeline

1921   Ireland is partitioned into the Irish Free State and Northern Ireland.

1928   Hasan al-Banna founds the Muslim Brotherhood Society in Egypt.

1939-1945   World War II takes place.

1945   Thousands of Jewish Holocaust survivors emigrate to British-controlled Palestine. The United Nations (UN) is founded.

1948   The State of Israel is created.

1949   The North Atlantic Treaty Organization (NATO) is established.

1951   Israeli prime minister David Ben-Gurion creates the Mossad.

1957   Israel's Sayeret Mat'kal is created.

1959   Basque students in Spain form the Euzkadi ta Askatasuna (ETA).

1964   The Palestinian Liberation Organization (PLO) is founded.

1967   The Six-Day War takes place. Israel occupies the West Bank. George Habash forms the Popular Front for the Liberation of Palestine (PFLP).

1969   The original Irish Republican Army splinters, leading to the creation of the Provisional Irish Republican Army (PIRA).

1970   Jordanian troops assault Palestinian refugee camps, an event that becomes known as Black September.

1971   Jordan's Counter Terrorist Battalion 71 (CTB-71) is created.

1972   Black September terrorists kill 11 Israeli athletes at the Munich Olympic Games. West Germany's Grenzschutzgruppe 9 (GSG-9) is created. The Netherlands' Bijzondere Bijstands Eenheid (BBE) is created. Sayeret Mat'kal rescues Sabena airline passengers from Black September hijackers.

1973   Palestinian terrorists seize the Saudi embassy in Paris, France. Israel's Ya'ma'm is created.

1974   France's Groupe d'Intervention de la Gendarmerie Nationale (GIGN) is created. Sayeret Mat'kal deploys to Israel's Ma'alot High School. The Soviet Union creates the Alpha Group.

1975   Spanish dictator Francisco Franco dies.

1976   The British Special Air Service (SAS) deploys to Northern Ireland after PIRA attacks increase. Sayeret Mat'kal deploys to Entebbe, Uganda, on a raid against PFLP and RAF hijackers.

1977   In Mogadishu, Somalia, GSG-9 rescues hostages from Red Army Faction (RAF) and Palestinian hijackers. Spain's Grupo Especiale para los Operaciones (GEO) is created. Egyptian president Anwar al-Sadat begins peace talks with Israel. Egypt's Force 777 is created.

1978   Italy's Gruppo Intervento Speciale (GIS) and Nucleo Centrale Operativo di Sicurezza (NOCS) are created. Fatah terrorists hijack a bus near Tel Aviv, killing 37 hostages before being killed themselves by Ya'ma'm.

1979   The GIGN and the Saudi National Guard end a terrorist takeover of the Grand Mosque in Mecca, Saudi Arabia.

1980   The British SAS carries out Operation Nimrod in London, England.

1981   Anwar al-Sadat is assassinated.

1982   The NOCS rescues U.S. Army brigadier general James Dozier from the Red Brigades. The British SAS deploys to the South Atlantic Ocean during the Falklands War. Osama bin Laden begins to organize al-Qaeda.

1985   Abu Nidal Organization (ANO) terrorists hijack an Egypt Air flight to Malta. Force 777's rescue mission ends in disaster. Colombia's Agrupacion de Fuerzas Especiales Anti-Terroristas Urbanas (AFEAU) is created. India's National Security Guards (NSG) is created.

1987   Sheikh Ahmed Yassin forms Hamas.

1988   Fatah terrorists hijack the "Bus of Mothers" in southern Israel. Israel gives up its claims to the West Bank.

1991   The Soviet Union collapses. Poland's Grupa Reagowania Operacyjno Mobilnego (GROM) is created.

1992   The Taliban seizes power in Afghanistan. Civil war breaks out in Bosnia.

1993   Canada's Joint Task Force 2 (JTF-2) is created.

1994   The GIGN rescues hostages on an Air France flight hijacked by Algerian terrorists. GSG-9 is embroiled in a scandal after an RAF stakeout. Hamas carries out its first major suicide bombings inside Israel.

1997   Communist rebels in Lima, Peru, take over the Japanese ambassador's residence. The Fuerza de Operaciones Especiales (FOE) rescues the hostages.

2000   The al-Aqsa Intifadah begins.

2001   Al-Qaeda terrorists attack the United States. Special forces from a U.S.-led coalition are deployed to Afghanistan against the Taliban and al-Qaeda.

2002   Alpha Group is deployed when Chechen rebels take over a Moscow theater. The rescue mission results in the deaths of many hostages. Al-Qaeda bombs a popular nightclub in Bali, Indonesia.

2003   Special forces from the U.S.-led coalition are deployed to Iraq.

2004   Terrorists bomb commuter trains in Madrid, Spain. Hamas leader Ahmed Yassin is killed in the Gaza Strip.

SELECTED BIBLIOGRAPHY

Bernard, Michael. *GIGN: Le Temps d'un Secret.* Paris: Bibliophile, 2003.

Dobson, Christopher, and Ronald Payne. *Counterattack: The West's Battle Against the Terrorists.* New York: Facts on File, 1982.

Gal, Reuven. *Portrait of the Israeli Soldier.* Westport, CT: Greenwood Press, 1986.

Geraghty, Tony. *Who Dares Wins: The Special Air Service—1950 to the Gulf War.* London: Bantam Books, 1992.

Harnden, Toby. *Bandit Country: The IRA and South Armagh.* Edinburgh: Hodder and Sloughton, 1999.

Katz, Samuel M. *The Elite.* New York: Pocket Books, 1992.

———. *The Hunt for the Engineer: How Israeli Agents Tracked the Hamas Master Bomber.* New York: Fromm, 1999.

Ladd, James D. *SBS: The Invisible Raiders.* London: Arms and Armour Press, 1983.

McNab, Andy. *Bravo Two Zero: The True Story of an SAS Patrol Behind the Lines in Iraq.* London: Bantam Press, 1993.

Micheletti, Eric. *Le GIGN en Action.* Paris: Histoire et Collections, 1997.

Tophoven, Rolf. *GSG 9: Kommando Gegen Terrorismus.* Munich: Bernard & Graefe, 1988.

Urban, Mark. *Big Boys' Rules: The Secret Struggle Against the IRA.* London: Faber and Faber, 1992.

Zonder, Moshe. *Sayeret Mat'kal.* Tel Aviv: Keter Publishing House Ltd., 2000.

FURTHER READING AND WEBSITES

Books

Currie, Stephen. *Terrorists and Terrorist Groups.* San Diego: Lucent Books, 2002.

Katz, Sam. *Against All Odds: Counterterrorist Hostage Rescues.* Minneapolis: Lerner Publications Company, 2005.

————. *At Any Cost: National Liberation Terrorism.* Minneapolis: Lerner Publications Company, 2004.

————. *Jerusalem or Death: Palestinian Terrorism.* Minneapolis: Lerner Publications Company, 2004.

————. *Jihad: Islamic Fundamentalist Terrorism.* Minneapolis: Lerner Publications Company, 2004.

————. *Raging Within: Ideological Terrorism.* Minneapolis: Lerner Publications Company, 2004.

————. *Targeting Terror: Counterterrorist Raids.* Minneapolis: Lerner Publications Company, 2005.

————. *U.S. Counterstrike: American Counterterrorism.* Minneapolis: Lerner Publications Company, 2005.

Kushner, Harvey W. *Encyclopedia of Terrorism.* Newbury Park, CA: Sage Publications, 2003.

Websites

BBC News:World Edition
<http://news.bbc.co.uk>
This website offers extensive international coverage and analysis of news and events.

CNN.com
<http://www.cnn.com>
This site provides the lastest news on world conflicts and terrorism.

International Policy Institute for Counter-Terrorism
<http://www.ict.org.il>
This site features up-to-date news and commentary on international terrorism, as well a sections on terrorist organizations and the Arab-Israeli conflict.

U.S. Department of State Counterterrorism Office
<http://www.state.gov/s/ct>
The U.S. government maintains this site offering information on historic and active terrorist groups.

INDEX

ABOUT THE AUTHOR

Samuel M. Katz is an expert in the field of international terrorism and counterterrorism, military special operations, and law enforcement. He has written more than 20 books and dozens of articles on these subjects, as well as creating documentaries and giving lectures to law enforcement and counterterrorist agencies around the world. The Terrorist Dossiers series is his first foray into the field of nonfiction for young people.

PHOTO ACKNOWLEDGMENTS

The images in this book are used with the permission of: © Samuel M. Katz, pp. 6, 17, 19, 20, 29, 32, 34, 44, 46, 47, 55, 56, 60; © Bettmann/CORBIS, pp. 11, 31; © Reuters NewMedia Inc./CORBIS, pp. 13, 41; © PARROT PASCAL/CORBIS SYGMA, p. 15; © BOSSU REGIS/CORBIS SYGMA, p. 21; © Robin Adshead/The Military Picture Library/CORBIS, pp. 23, 24; © Hulton|Archive by Getty Images, pp. 27, 53; © AFP/Getty Images, pp. 35, 57; © Hulton-Deutsch/CORBIS, p. 39; © Kevin Fleming/CORBIS, p. 40; © Israel Government Press Office, p. 48; © Getty Images, pp. 50, 61, 63; AP/Wide World Photos, p. 59; © Rufo/Action Press/ZUMA, p. 62. Front cover ©Tony Linck/Time Life Pictures/Getty Images.

DATE DUE